king on the court:
BILLIE JEAN KING

Author

Leila Boyle Gemme

Photography

Bruce Curtis

 RAINTREE EDITIONS

Published by   **Raintree Editions**
A Division of Raintree Publishers Limited
Milwaukee, Wisconsin 53203

Distributed by   Childrens Press
1224 West Van Buren Street
Chicago, Illinois 60607

Library of Congress Cataloging in Publication Data

Gemme, Leila B.
    King on the court.

    SUMMARY: A biography of the tennis champion
who has done much to assure an equal place for women
in professional tennis.
    1. King, Billie Jean—Juvenile literature.
2. Tennis—Juvenile literature. [1. King, Billie Jean.
2. Tennis—Biography] I. Curtis, Bruce. II. Title.
GV994.K56G45   796.34′2′0924 [B] [92]   75-42488
ISBN 0-8172-0129-7
ISBN 0-8172-0128-9 lib. bdg.

Contents

To Mother and Father

Going Out on a High

Sweat beads up on her face. The rimless glasses glint in the sun. Billie Jean looks pressured.

The first set has gone badly; she lost it 2-6 to Chris Evert. Around her the Wimbledon crowd peers in near silence. They know, because Billie Jean has said it publicly, that this 1975 tournament is her final major singles match. At 31 she wants to devote her time to team tennis.

But first she wants this match — badly. She hates losing more than anything in the world. "Victory is fleeting," she has written, "but losing is forever." It is an attitude that has shaped her whole life.

The crowd stirs. It looks like the end is near. She wins the second set of this semifinal match after a slow start. But now she is three games down in the third set. Billie Jean looks grim.

But the magic returns. The flashy aggressiveness is back. There is little that Chris Evert can do against Billie Jean at her best. The set ends 6-3 for Billie Jean, and her singles career still has a few more hours to go.

Finals day dawns — July 4th. Billie Jean hasn't spent an Independence Day at home in years. Maybe next year. But today she must face the young Australian,

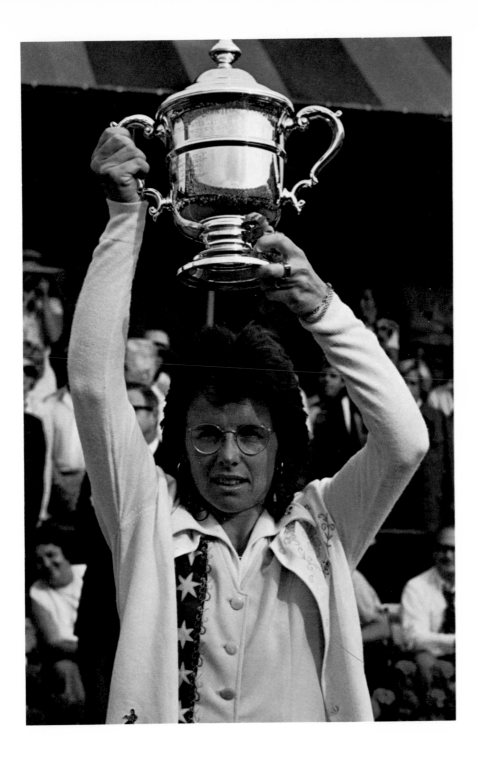

Evonne Goolagong Cawley.

The finals match is over in 39 minutes. The score is nearly perfect: 6-0, 6-1. Billie Jean King is again, for the sixth time, the singles champion at Wimbledon.

After the match the reporters come. "I wanted to go out on a high," she rejoices to them, "and I did. I have never worked harder, trained harder. I have never thought so much about it. I just did everything in my power to win." It would never occur to Billie Jean King to do otherwise. Playing to win has been one of the most important goals in her life.

Every year since her first Wimbledon match in 1961, Billie Jean has visited the stadium when it was empty. It is a beautiful place — stately, dignified, but not terribly stuffy. Empty, the green of the grass court and the ivy-covered grandstand is warm and inviting. It is a place that makes tennis seem very important.

Billie Jean adores the place. "I just love it here," she said during the 1975 tournament. "I love that Centre Court. I wish I could hug it sometimes."

Perhaps she loves it so much because it has lived up to her childhood dreams. Much of tennis hasn't. The stuffy, upper class atmosphere of the game drove her wild. The antifemale bias was unbearable. But her dreams of Wimbledon did not exceed the reality.

At Wimbledon in 1975 she could look back on an unequaled career. She was at the top of her profession. And much of what she won, she won here, at the Lawn Tennis Championships known simply as Wimbledon.

Winning

Billie Jean first came to Wimbledon in 1961. She was
Billie Jean Moffitt then, a chunky 17-year-old from California.
An unknown. She and her friend, Karen Hantze, roomed
together in an old boarding house. It cost $1.20 a night
including breakfast. They giggled a lot and ate too much.
And they surprised everybody — perhaps even themselves
— by taking the women's doubles.

Billie Jean was thrilled, but she was really after the singles
title. And she was determined to get it.

The next year at Wimbledon, Billie Jean Moffitt made
her name, but not by winning the singles. In the second
round she was scheduled to play the Australian,
Margaret Smith (later Margaret Court). Smith's reputation
was already made. She was the number one woman player.

The match was to be played on Centre Court, the most
important court at Wimbledon. Billie Jean was thrilled. She
loved Centre Court even then, and she was dying to play
Margaret Smith. Sportswriters gave her no chance at all.

The first set confirmed the sportswriters' views. Margaret
won easily, 6-1. But in the second set, the game reversed.
Billie Jean went far ahead and took the set 6-3.

Centre Court was jammed with people anxious to see

an upset. The crowd fell deadly silent during the third set as Billie Jean fell farther and farther behind. Then, with Margaret just two points from winning, Billie Jean bore down. Her nervousness seemed to disappear, and a cool, deadly, aggressive instinct took over. Within a few minutes, she had defeated Margaret Smith. The crowd went wild. It was an upset like no other. For the first time in the entire history of Wimbledon, the top woman player had been ousted in her first round. Overnight, Billie Jean Moffitt was famous in tennis circles.

But it didn't mean the singles crown. She was defeated in the quarterfinals that year. She would have to wait until 1966 for the singles victory she wanted so much.

In the years between her tremendous upset of Margaret Smith and her first Wimbledon singles victory, life changed in many ways for Billie Jean Moffitt.

She entered college in California, but dropped out three years later.

She made a decision to devote herself fully to tennis — to "becoming number one."

She went to Australia for special tennis lessons with Mervyn Rose.

And she married Larry King.

In 1966, Billie Jean returned to Wimbledon with a new last name and a fresh approach to her game. She breezed through the first week of play, not playing at top form but winning anyway.

On finals day she faced Maria Bueno, a Brazilian player noted for her graceful style. Maria Bueno had been the Wimbledon singles champion three times. Billie Jean was tense. She was as close to her goal as she had ever been.

She easily won the first set. Her plan worked perfectly.

Billie Jean hit wide to Maria's forehand and chopped her returns at Maria's feet. Her lobs were superb. There was little the Brazilian could do. Billie Jean took the set 6-3.

Maria came back in the second set. She won 6-3, and kept her advantage through the first two games of the third set. But Billie Jean's dream was not about to end unhappily this time. Suddenly her tennis was so tough and so perfect that Maria could only shrug as she missed even easy shots. The third set ended 6-3, and Billie Jean threw her racket skyward.

She had done it at last, after six years of trying. Wimbledon fans who had followed her long struggle were overjoyed. Princess Marina — president of the Wimbledon Association — presented Billie Jean with the symbolic silver tray as the crowd shouted its delight.

In the years that followed, Billie Jean King had glorious victories and bitter disappointments. She repeated her Wimbledon singles victory in 1967 and 1968. In 1967 she also won the women's doubles and the mixed doubles at Wimbledon, and took the U.S. Open at Forest Hills.

She was clearly a winner, and undeniably number one among the active players. Yet something was missing. For all her success, tennis writers and critics refused to give her the credit she deserved. They would admit that she was good, but never as good as champions of the past. Never the best. It irked Billie Jean to no end.

Also, Billie Jean learned that fans are fickle. On the way up they loved her. But after a few major victories, she became the champion in their eyes, and their sympathies turned to the underdog. It was hard to take.

The late '60s were tough years for Billie Jean. Poor health forced her out of competition for many months. She has athlete's knees. They are great for sports because they help an athlete run and change directions quickly. But they

are prone to injury. She also had trouble with the tennis establishment. Her dream of being fully accepted as the number one player seemed as far away as ever.

But in the early '70s, Billie Jean's career brightened. She took Forest Hills in 1971, 1972, and 1974. Wimbledon was hers again in 1972, 1973, and 1975. She emerged as a leader in the revolution that overtook tennis in the late '60s and early '70s. And, at last, sportswriters and the tennis establishment began to acknowledge that Billie Jean King was the best — maybe the best ever in women's tennis.

Part of Billie Jean's fantastic success is due to her great natural talent. Part of the credit goes to her expert coaches. But much of it is a result of her gritty determination to be a winner. "Defeat is something I just can't seem to get rid of. It never leaves my insides," she said in her autobiography.

This kind of determination has meant hours and years on a tennis court. It has meant days and months with little or no time for relaxation. It has meant an unusual, long-distance marriage to the man she loves.

But it is the way Billie Jean King has wanted it from the beginning. Looking back from her final Wimbledon victory in 1975, she has few regrets. She is happy with her career, with its many successes. And she looks forward to the growth of team tennis, her new interest. In the warm flush of her sixth Wimbledon singles victory, she told reporters, "I think I am the most fortunate woman athlete who ever lived."

Getting There

Billie Jean Moffitt was ten years old when she took her first tennis lesson. It was a short lesson given by Clyde Walker, tennis instructor for the city of Long Beach.

After it was over, Billie Jean stayed on for several hours to practice what she had learned. When her mother arrived at the court, the sweaty, pudgy little girl jumped into the car. "Mom, I know what I want to be," she announced. "I want to be the number one tennis player in the world."

Billie Jean Moffitt had played sports almost since she could walk. Sandlot football and baseball were her favorites. And she was good. Her father, Bill Moffitt, worked for the fire department. At department picnics, everyone wanted Billie Jean on his team. Every day after school she played until dinner time. But her parents worried that baseball and football would not offer her much chance to play as an adult. They urged her to find a more "ladylike" sport.

Billie Jean asked her father about possible sports. He suggested golf, swimming, or tennis. The first two didn't interest her much. But she loved running and hard exercise, so she thought tennis might be the answer.

There was, however, the problem of getting a racket. The Moffitts weren't wealthy, and they believed that kids should work for what they want. So Billie Jean did odd jobs

around the neighborhood until she saved the $8 she needed.

The young tennis player soon learned that her goal of becoming number one was not easily reached. Tennis is a complex game involving a great variety of strokes. To become really good, you must learn them all. And that takes time. Billie Jean has always been an impatient person with an overwhelmingly competitive nature. She wanted to play and to win — immediately! When things didn't go her way, she could unleash a very bad temper.

"I couldn't stand to lose," she has said of that period. "It used to just *kill* me. But I felt in the long run that if I really wanted to achieve my goals I would *have* to lose."

In spite of the frustrations, Billie Jean kept at it. She played tennis every day, and even followed Clyde Walker from court to court around Long Beach to get more lessons. To strengthen her legs, she walked the three miles back and forth to school each day. Some days she would spend hours working on just one shot.

Billie Jean was serious about her goal. She went to school, made friends, carried on a normal life. But her day never really began until three o'clock, when she could head for the courts to practice tennis.

During her teenage years, Billie Jean got a chance to study under Alice Marble. Marble had been a tennis great in the '30s. Clyde Walker encouraged Billie Jean to take the opportunity. He felt that Marble's coaching would improve her game. So every weekend, Billie Jean stayed with Alice Marble and practiced tennis under her direction. The former tennis star was impressed with Billie Jean's dedication. "She was so crazy about tennis I'd have to lock her in her room to study," she said of her young student.

During these early years, Billie Jean received help from a lot of people. Her parents, Clyde Walker, Alice Marble — all went out of their way to encourage her. They were impressed with her ambition. But there was at least one place that gave Billie Jean little help. That was the Southern California Lawn Tennis Association (SCLTA).

This group, headed by Perry Jones, was part of the United States Lawn Tennis Association (USLTA). It controlled amateur tennis in Southern California. It was supposed to aid younger players by setting up local tournaments and providing money for players to travel to tournaments in other areas.

But Billie Jean Moffitt never saw much of that money. The SCLTA catered to youngsters who played in private clubs. It helped those who knew the proper way to dress and act on the court. And most of its money went to promising male players.

The SCLTA officials weren't impressed by an outspoken fireman's daughter from the wrong side of the tracks in Long Beach. Fortunately for Billie Jean, a group of home town people known as the Long Beach Tennis Patrons came to her aid. They frequently put up the money that allowed her to travel to tournaments in other states. But Billie Jean did not forget her resentment of the SCLTA. Many years later it would change her career and help to change the entire structure of tennis.

Once she began to travel, Billie Jean met other people who were willing to help her. In New Jersey, a tennis coach named Frank Brennan was impressed with her play. After one tournament he approached the young player.

"Why do you play with nylon instead of gut?" Brennan asked, referring to the strings on Billie Jean's racket.

"Can't afford gut," said Billie Jean simply.

Brennan sent her some gut strings and soon was coaching her whenever she came to New Jersey. He taught her a lot about planning tournament games. And he has continued to coach her on and off throughout her career. In fact, in 1973, Frank Brennan was one of the people who helped Billie Jean get ready for the most spectacular match of her career; the Bobby Riggs match, the famed "Battle of the Sexes."

Although Brennan helped her greatly during the mid-1960s, Billie Jean still felt that her game lacked something. She was a top-ranked player, but she wasn't winning major tournaments. She was in college, which meant that she had to give up serious tennis for nearly eight months of the year.

Finally Billie Jean decided that if she was ever going to be number one, she had to give up everything but tennis.

She dropped out of school, and in the fall of 1964 she made arrangements to go to Australia for more coaching.

It was a particularly difficult decision because Billie Jean had just become engaged to a fellow student named Larry King. But Larry thought she should go. He wanted her to fulfill her ambitions.

When she left for Australia, Billie Jean announced her intentions to the press. "I am leaving to become the number one player in the world, and I can't do that and go to school at the same time."

Later she admitted that she was scared. It was one thing to go quietly with a secret ambition. But with the whole world knowing her intentions, Billie Jean knew she wouldn't be able to fail quietly. If she fell on her face, she knew she would have quite an audience.

In Australia, Billie Jean studied under famed coach Mervyn Rose. He put her through long, tedious daily work-outs. He changed her serve and her ground strokes. This completely threw Billie Jean for a while. Her game went to pieces until she mastered the new shots. She lost matches to children. She could barely serve at all. For stamina, Rose had her play two players at a time. At first she could last only a few minutes against two players. Eventually she was able to go for an hour or more.

The results of Billie Jean's three months in Australia did not show up right away. It took her several months more to master the new techniques, and it was a full year before she could see the change in her game.

Along with the changes in her game came an important realization. Billie Jean recognized the need for the "killer instinct."

Many champions talk about the killer instinct. Rod Laver, the Australian great, devotes a section of his book on tennis to it. The killer instinct separates championship players from very good players who are not champion caliber. It is the ability to recognize key points of a match and keep the pressure on the opponent. It involves staying relaxed enough to be able to survive mistakes and still keep pushing the opposition.

Maureen Connelly, the late tennis star of the '50s, said of Billie Jean, "What she has is that rare ability to rise to the necessary pressure threshold and stay there for the big ones — those moments when it's 30-all and you've missed the first serve and have to get the second one in. Billie can get it in."

One good example of Billie Jean's killer instinct in action was the women's singles final at Wimbledon in 1972. Billie Jean wanted this one badly. The year before, Evonne Goolagong had beaten her in the semifinals. And Evonne and Chris Evert had snared the lion's share of attention in the press that year.

Billie Jean said she started practicing for 1972 when she "shook hands with Evonne" after the 1971 match.

In 1972 she again faced Evonne, this time in the finals. The Australian was clearly favored by the crowd, but Billie Jean didn't seem to notice.

She stood in Centre Court that July day paying attention only to the game. Several bad line calls didn't appear to faze her. She concentrated on Evonne. Her game was quick, neat, brilliant. It was over fast: 6-3, 6-3. And Billie Jean was champion at Wimbledon again.

Some people said it would have been good for tennis for a younger player to win in 1972. Billie Jean scoffed at the idea. "I've waited a whole 363 days to make up for my last Wimbledon," she said. "I'm not about to lie down and lose for a storybook."

Obviously, Billie Jean's killer instinct works for her much

more often than not. But there are times when it
doesn't. Mostly, these are times when she lets her temper
and impatience get control.

During one period of her career, Billie Jean's emotions
tended to interfere with the concentration necessary to
make the kill. Late in 1965, the United States Lawn Tennis
Association proposed that Billie Jean be ranked number
one among female tennis players. But at the USLTA
meeting in February, 1966, the Texas delegation, led by
Al Bumann, argued that the clay court champion,
Nancy Richey, should be ranked first. The organization
finally compromised and co-ranked them as first.
Billie Jean was furious and frustrated.

At Forest Hills that September, she was dying to play against
Richey and settle the matter. The world of tennis was
eager for this match, too. Male star Clark Graebner declared,
"If those two play against each other at Forest Hills,
I'd walk from Cleveland to New York to watch."

At the tournament, Billie Jean was scheduled to play
Australian Kerry Melville in the second round. Walking onto
the court, Billie Jean discovered that one of the line judges
was Al Bumann. She angrily demanded his withdrawal.
The Forest Hills officials refused, and Bumann
refused to step down.

Billie Jean played the match, but it was a disaster. She
blew her cool completely. She hit every shot with all her
power and lost in straight sets.

When she finally faced Nancy Richey two years later, she
fared no better. Playing on clay, Richey's favorite surface,
Billie Jean fell apart. Of the final 51 points scored,
Billie Jean won only 12.

In spite of these occasional lapses, Billie Jean's killer
instinct has worked well for her since the mid-'60s — even
during the intense political conflict that plagued tennis
in the last years of that decade.

Changing Tennis

On a warm June day in 1955, Billie Jean Moffitt set out for her first real tennis tournament. She was a little nervous and very excited. She had been taking lessons from Clyde Walker for only a few months, and here she was on her way to a tournament run by the Southern California Lawn Tennis Association!

At the posh Los Angeles Tennis Club where the tournament was held, Billie Jean won her first round and lost her second. But the outcome of that first match was not very important. Something else that happened that day was to have lasting impact.

When the young players gathered for a photograph, Perry Jones, the SCLTA director, told Billie Jean to step aside. Surprised, she did so. He then told her that she couldn't be in the picture because she was wearing shorts and a shirt — not a proper tennis dress.

Billie Jean could hardly believe it. She couldn't understand why dressing a certain way should matter in a tennis match. It was one of the attitudes of the Lawn Tennis Associations that would continue to bother her.

In those early years, Billie Jean discovered many things that she did not like about the way tennis was run. Important tournaments almost always were held in private clubs.

Her parents, not club members themselves, didn't enjoy the atmosphere of those places.

Tennis tournaments were nothing like other sports events. No hawkers sold hot dogs; nobody cheered or booed. It was all very quiet, very correct, very expensive. There was nothing there to interest what Billie Jean called the "average guy." No big prizes were at stake. No fans loudly supported one player or another.

Nobody will ever know for sure why Billie Jean became the rebel that she did.

Perhaps Perry Jones really hurt her that day, although she has said he did not.

Perhaps her pastor influenced her. Billie Jean's church was run by the Rev. Bob Richards, an outstanding former Olympic athlete. Maybe his teaching taught her to fight for her principles.

Maybe it was the influence of her parents.

Or, perhaps, Billie Jean's own personality made her different.

Whatever the cause, she knew that some things were wrong with tennis. And, from the beginning, she knew she wanted to change the face of the game. This desire would regularly cause friction between her and the crusty establishment of the sport she loved.

One of the early problems stemmed from Billie Jean's style of play. Most of the other female players were "baseliners" who played toward the back of the court. It was the acceptable form for women. Billie Jean's net-rushing, serve-and-volley game wasn't appreciated by the stuffier members of the USLTA.

Tennis critics denounced her for it. One paper referred to her "gym teacher style," and she was frequently criticized for "playing like a man." Never mind her success — her style was all wrong for a woman.

Even after her fabulous success in the mid-'60s, few tennis leaders would give her credit. She was good, they said, but not as good as Helen Wills Moody, or Alice Marble, or Maureen Connelly, or Margaret Court. In fact, when Billie Jean won her first Wimbledon in 1966, Martin Tressel, president of the USLTA at the time, stated that if Maria Bueno had not been off her game, Billie Jean wouldn't have won.

The USLTA did not like Billie Jean very much, and they weren't going to give her any more credit than they had to.

But it wasn't just Billie Jean's style that bothered tennis chieftains. Her manner on the court drove them mad, too. Throughout her early career, Billie Jean's mouth moved as fast as her racket.

"Move, you ox," she'd yell to get herself going. Or, when things were really bad, "Throw in your nickels and dimes, folks, this is the worst show on earth."

This talk doesn't sound bad in the '70s, but in the mid-'60s tennis was still very dignified, very upper class. Billie Jean's fans loved her court antics, but the USLTA was not amused by them. Often she was warned to stop and threatened with punishment if she did not.

Later Billie Jean did stop her chatter, but only because she thought it hurt her concentration and her game. However, she didn't stop arguing with tournament officials.

"Hey!" she would yell to them when a bad call displeased her. One time she challenged an official. "How can you see from there?" she shouted. He ignored the remark, but when he thought no one was looking, he moved his chair to get a better view.

Billie Jean resented the attitude of the USLTA toward her language and actions. In one interview she protested to a reporter. "In basketball and football the players are cussing out there like troopers," she said. "But if you're a tennis player, you've got to be jolly nice all the time."

In fact, it was Billie Jean's public statements that upset the USLTA most in the decade of the '60s. Only a few players had ever tried to break away from the organization, and they had not been very successful. Almost the only form of protest a player had was a public statement. Billie Jean was never shy about public statements.

Once, in Chicago, a reporter asked to interview her for the women's section of the paper. "That's the trouble with this sport," she burst out at the surprised journalist. "We've got to get it off the society pages and onto the sports pages."

In another interview in 1967, she struck out at the whole image of the game. "We desperately need to revamp the image of tennis," she said. "It's too prissy and too white — no swearing, no cheering by the crowd during play, too identified with private clubs and mint juleps."

Billie Jean did a lot of thinking and speaking about her sport during her early playing years. She decided that the major problem in tennis was its status as an amateur sport. Until 1968, there were no teams or leagues in tennis. No tournaments offered prize money for winners.

Instead, each player was a member of a national association. For players in the United States, this was the USLTA. The USLTA and the national associations of other countries provided players with expense and travel money.

In the United States, expense money was supposed to be limited to $28 a day. But good players could get more.

Tournament directors needed top players to help attract big crowds. So they would approach the stars and offer money in excess of the $28. It wasn't against the law, but it wasn't aboveboard either. Billie Jean hated it.

The system, she felt, kept many people out of the game. Players on the way up received only minimum expense money. They couldn't afford to live on this small amount and still devote full time to tennis.

This meant that tennis was restricted to people who could afford it. The only poor people who could compete were those who became stars almost as soon as they started. It also meant that the people who ran tennis were wealthy amateurs. The officiating was amateur, and often not very good.

By 1967, many other tennis players shared Billie Jean's views. Most of them didn't talk about it in public, though. Billie Jean did.

She said that the whole amateur system was ridiculous. She told people that there were no real amateurs in the sport, because under the expense system, everybody was getting paid.

The USLTA shuddered a collective shudder. Officials warned Billie Jean that she was going to be in trouble if she didn't learn to keep her mouth shut. But, of course, she didn't.

Then some male tennis players decided to form a professional league. It had been tried unsuccessfully before. But this time many top players joined. They signed contracts to earn regular salaries. Prizes were given to winners of their tournaments. It looked like a good chance to make the sport truly professional.

The national associations were horrified. They ruled that none of the professionals could play in major tournaments like Wimbledon and Forest Hills.

The players were faced with a difficult decision. If they turned professional, they could probably make a good living at their sport. But only if they remained amateurs could they compete in the most important tournaments in tennis.

Billie Jean knew what she wanted to do. Early in 1968, she became the first of four women tennis players to become professional athletes. She signed a contract with the National Tennis League, headed by George MacCall.

Slowly, the national associations began to change their minds about professional tennis. Too many top players were turning pro. If they continued to exclude pros from their tournaments, they would be left mainly with second-rate players. Their tournaments would be less exciting, and fewer people would attend.

Finally, the national associations changed their policies. They began open tennis, in which amateur and professional players competed against each other. With this change, tennis gained a much larger audience than it had known before. Prize money skyrocketed, and the general public began to take notice.

Billie Jean was happy with these changes. She had been urging something like this for years. Now she could be a professional and still compete in major tournaments.

Billie Jean's life as a professional was very busy. The members of the National Tennis League were touring pros. They traveled around the world, sometimes playing in a different town or city each night. Playing conditions were often poor. It was grueling work. But for Billie Jean, it was a good experience. And she was earning a good living at tennis.

Billie Jean King has often been criticized for her interest in money. She talks about it a lot and worked hard in 1971 to become the first female athlete to earn over $100,000 in a single year. She insists that it's not just the money that interests her. She and her husband Larry live rather simply. She believes money is important, though, because other people think it is. When people hear about a $100,000-a-year player, they take notice. They decide to go out and see her play. As Billie Jean once put it, "Making one hundred grand is the way to America's consciousness."

Billie Jean is rich and famous now. But she's never forgotten what it was like to be a kid off the public courts. Fortunately, when Billie Jean was growing up in Long Beach, there was good public tennis instruction there. But she knew that few towns offered that, and tennis instruction in public schools was even more rare. City kids and poor kids were practically excluded from the game; black children were almost completely absent from tennis. Only two or three black people had ever made it to the top of the sport.

Throughout her career, Billie Jean donated her time to coaching kids whenever she had the chance. She'd go to

public parks and city recreational areas to teach.

"Keep your left foot forward and practice every day," were her regular instructions. If there was time, she'd get into the fundamentals of grip and ground strokes. But it was never enough.

So, in the early '70s, she, Larry, and tennis pro Dennis Van Der Meer began a series of tennis camps called TennisAmerica. The goal of the company was to bring tennis to lots of people who didn't have much opportunity to learn how to play.

Today, TennisAmerica is only part of a wider tennis boom that has hit the United States. More and more people want to play. Many tennis camps have opened. Towns and cities all over the country are building public courts. Tennis is no longer an upper class, country club diversion, but a sport of the middle class. Part of Billie Jean's dream for tennis has been fulfilled.

The most recent area of change in which Billie Jean is deeply involved is World Team Tennis (WTT). WTT features tennis teams in various cities around the country. Men's and women's singles, men's and women's doubles, and mixed doubles are played. The teams play against each other for a championship — not unlike baseball.

Billie Jean is enthusiastic about WTT. "America is tuned into team sports," she says. "I've always wanted to bring tennis to the masses." WTT uses a different form of the game. The scoring system has been simplified. Matches are played in big arenas like Madison Square Garden. And the fans get to yell and cheer for their favorites. In other words, it has many of the characteristics Billie Jean always said tennis needed—even when she was a little girl.

Changing Society

Billie Jean prowled nervously around her Houston hotel room. She devoured candy bars and gulped Gatorade. In just one hour, she would be playing the most celebrated match of her life. And the importance of it had just hit her full force.

If she lost, much of what she had spent her life working for would be gone. It was a terrifying thought. She wished the thought away and concentrated on her plans for the game. She closed her eyes and brought up memories of the films of Bobby Riggs. Suddenly she knew she could do it. She *had* to do it!

It had all begun weeks before. On Mother's Day, 1973, Riggs had humiliated Margaret Court in a colorful "Battle of the Sexes" match. Billie Jean wanted to avenge that loss. The honor of women's tennis demanded it.

Riggs, a 55-year-old ex-tennis champion, constantly berated women's tennis. Women were too soft, too gutless to play good tennis, he said. They crumpled under fire.

Billie Jean had worked too hard as an athlete to let him continue that kind of talk, even if Riggs wasn't serious. Bobby Riggs was a hustler and a gambler. Much of what he said was surely for publicity. He wanted to get people interested in his matches and make the stakes higher. But

for Billie Jean, a match with Riggs was more than a big promotional scheme. When she agreed to play him, she really felt that she was laying much of her career on the line.

The King-Riggs match involved an enormous amount of money — $100,000 for the winner plus extras from advertising and promotion. Billie Jean's money-hungry image came back to haunt her. But she didn't care. She felt that unless the match involved a great amount of money, nobody would take it seriously.

All kinds of publicity gimmicks preceded the match. Riggs' talk grew worse than ever. And this night — September 20, 1973 — Billie Jean understood how much she wanted to win this one.

The noise in the Astrodome was deafening. Fans yelled and screamed; music blared. It looked more like a college football championship or the World Series than a tennis match. Billie Jean loved it. Tennis was finally, thoroughly, out of the country club. The "average guy" she had always wanted for a fan was there. And 40 million more "average guys" watched on television.

The match itself was less difficult than she had imagined. Riggs seemed out of condition. His lack of speed surprised her. Once in the first set he broke her service and surged

ahead 3-2. Riggs fans were elated; this was the moment of truth.

Billie Jean came back immediately and took the first set 6-4. She didn't even look winded.

The next two sets were all downhill for Bobby Riggs. His famous soft shots—lobs and spins—failed him completely. Billie Jean was everywhere. She easily returned shots he never thought she could make.

In the end it was a decisive win: 6-4, 6-3, 6-3. Elated, Billie Jean accepted the victory check to the shattering roar of the crowd.

For Billie Jean King, the Riggs match was the highpoint in her latest fight. After gaining championship status and participating in the "pro revolution," Billie Jean soon had another crusade on her hands.

The acceptance of professionals in tennis had changed some aspects of the game. Acceptance of money was open and aboveboard now. The phony amateur days were over. But all was not well.

The main problem was prize money. Prize money in tournaments often was vastly different for men and women players. Sometimes, first prize for men's singles was ten times the amount that women received. It made Billie Jean furious. In May of 1970, she played in the Italian Open. First prize for the men was $7,500; first prize for the women was $600. "That's when I began thinking boycott," she said later.

There were many other things that bothered Billie Jean and other women players.

Facilities were one problem. Women's dressing rooms were usually inferior to men's. While many tournaments offered masseurs for the men, only a few offered this service to female athletes.

Court placement was a more serious matter. Only the most important women's matches were played at center court, the main arena at tennis tournaments. Men players usually had it all to themselves.

Press coverage was a sore point, too. No matter how important or exciting a women's match was, it was covered at the end of the tennis story. All the men's events, no matter how insignificant, were traditionally covered first. The final paragraph of a tennis story usually would begin, "And in women's tennis . . . ." It was insulting, and Billie Jean was determined to do something about it.

The first step was to attack the idea of unequal prize money. At the U.S. Open at Forest Hills in 1970, Billie Jean got the women players together to discuss the problems. The boycott she had thought about in Rome seemed about to become a reality. The women players were fed up. Ahead, on September 21, was the Pacific Southwest tournament. It offered first prize money of $12,500 for male players and $1,500 for the women. The women decided that they would not accept this. They talked to tennis writer Gladys Heldman about the situation. Heldman approached Jack Kramer, the Pacific Southwest tournament director, about equalizing the prize money. But he wouldn't do anything.

Instead of a boycott, the women players made a decision that changed the face of tennis. Through Gladys Heldman, they arranged an all-female tournament at Houston for September 21. It was called the Virginia Slims Invitational, and was sponsored by the cigarette company.
First prize was $7,500.

The USLTA was furious. The organization refused to give permission for the tournament, and suspended all the players who had agreed to play in Texas. This meant that the nine players who had signed would have to give up their idea or be willing to go off on their own, without the USLTA.

It was not an easy decision. If they stayed with the USLTA, the women could at least win some prize money and play in some regularly scheduled tournaments. Alone, they might not make it. Billie Jean worried particularly about the younger players whose reputations were not yet made.

Larry King advised his wife to go ahead with it. Only alone, Larry felt, could the women players really prove that they could attract crowds and be valuable to sponsors.

So the Virginia Slims tour, also known as "Women's Lob," began. Billie Jean and eight others signed contracts with

Gladys Heldman's *World Tennis* magazine. Virginia Slims agreed to sponsor a series of tournaments with the newly-formed women's professional group.

Billie Jean explained that money wasn't the only issue. "I got angry because women's tennis was being downgraded," she said. "I wanted recognition for women players. I think we draw as many spectators as men do."

The general reaction to the new tour was all bad. The USLTA maintained its suspensions. Male players called the idea of equal prize money ridiculous. And sportswriters hooted at the idea of a women's tour. Who would go to see them play?

Everyone did, as it turned out. "Women's Lob" was a smashing success. Prize money for women in the United States rose from under $50,000 in 1970 to better than $300,000 in 1971 for the Slims tour alone. Slims prize money in 1972 amounted to over half a million dollars. And in 1971, Billie Jean King became the first professional female athlete to make over $100,000 in a single year.

A few players were jealous of Billie Jean's success, but most appreciated her efforts. Looking back, player Tory Fretz said, "Billie Jean was more than the number one player. She was the impetus, she did the whole thing."

But the "whole thing" wasn't done yet.

The USLTA realized that the success of the separate women's tour could hurt its tournaments. So the suspensions were lifted and agreements reached. Basically, this meant that the Slims women could again play in major USLTA tournaments from which they had been banned.

But still, in many of these tournaments, the prize money remained unequal—improved but unequal. When Billie Jean won the U.S. Open in 1972, she got $10,000. Male star Ilie Nastase got $25,000 for the same victory in that tournament.

By 1973, even that had changed. U.S. Open officials at Forest Hills announced equal prize money for men and women. Other tournaments soon followed this action. It was a big victory for Billie Jean. The other players gave her a lot of the credit for it. "Everybody has Billie Jean to thank," Chris Evert said at the time.

Billie Jean King's interest in creating equality for women in tennis grew into a wider interest in women in all sports. As a woman athlete, she knew firsthand the pressures that girls who like athletics face. Her own sport was chosen because it was "ladylike."

Billie Jean knew that schools and towns rarely offered girls much in the form of athletics.

And she knew the attitude of the press. Reporters were always asking her the same questions: "When are you going to retire and have a baby?" "What does your husband think of your career?" She always wondered why reporters never asked men players the same kinds of questions.

Many people found the idea of women in sports unusual or unacceptable. Billie Jean King wanted to change that attitude.

At first she limited her actions to public statements about the difficulties women athletes faced. But, as in the past, speaking out was not enough.

In 1974, Billie Jean and Larry started a magazine, womenSports. It is devoted to female athletics. It carries articles about various women athletes who are rarely covered in other sports publications. The magazine has found a wide audience of readers who never had a publication devoted to their interests before.

The events in Billie Jean King's life have done much to change the idea that sports is a poor profession for women. She has achieved enormous financial success. She has helped to make tennis one of the fastest-growing sports in America. And after the Riggs match, Senator Hugh Scott of Pennsylvania said of her, "Billie Jean King has ratified the 28th Amendment." This proposed measure, also known as the Equal Rights Amendment, outlaws discrimination in all areas because of sex.

For her immediate goal, Billie Jean seeks acceptance of herself "as a woman who also happens to be an athlete." But the battle for full acceptance of female athletes is far from over. It is hard to believe that Billie Jean will rest until it is won. And it is even more difficult to imagine that she will not win it.

Living

There is a private Billie Jean King behind the woman
the world knows. She is a quieter, simpler woman
who likes music and books and walking on beaches.
After her final singles victory at Wimbledon she told
reporters, "Now I can have beer and ice cream again — you
have no idea how much I love the stuff."

Beer and ice cream, two of her favorite foods, are typical
of her tastes in many other things. "My idea of a gourmet
meal," she wrote once, "is a hamburger." For all the wealth
and glamour of her career, her tastes have remained
much the same as they were in Long Beach when she
was a little girl.

She loves simple foods, modern music, poetry, and the
movies. Her appearance and personality are very different
from what sports publicity sometimes suggests. In person
her features are more delicate, her voice softer. "She's
charming," new acquaintances will say in shock, as if they
had been expecting to meet the Wicked Witch of the West.

With no question, Billie Jean King's life has been very
different because of her career. She has had little time for
the simple pleasures that she loves. The urge to win
and the broadening demands of her career have consumed
most of her time.

Her long marriage to Larry is not an ordinary one. She is sometimes away more than half the year. The marriage has had its rough spots. Yet the Kings seem to have worked out their unusual arrangement to please themselves. Billie Jean has often said of Larry, "He's more women's lib than I am."

Billie Jean's career has made her world-famous. She has met kings and presidents. She has traveled more miles than she would like to remember.

Her career also has made her a subject of controversy. There are people within tennis who can't stand her. They see her as a loud-mouthed, money-hungry headline-seeker. But many others look up to her as the leader who has made tennis better for them all.

Part of that career is over now. The days of winning major singles battles ended in 1975 at Wimbledon, where they began so many years ago. She will play team tennis — she thinks it is the wave of the future. And, perhaps, she will play doubles. But the exciting, record-breaking singles contests are over.

She leaves tennis singles as the leading female player of her generation. In fact, she may be the greatest player of either sex of her era. She leaves, too, with the recognition, even from her enemies, that she is one of the all-time greats.

But it is hard to picture the words "retirement" and "Billie Jean King" in the same sentence. If the next phase of her life proves as sensational as the first, the world still has much to look forward to from Billie Jean.